GRANTHAM

A Pictorial History

The Tollemache Statue, 1897

GRANTHAM

A Pictorial History

Malcolm Knapp

Phillimore

1990

Published by
PHILLIMORE & CO. LTD.
Shopwyke Hall, Chichester, Sussex

ISBN 0 85033 728 3

Printed and bound in Great Britain by
BIDDLES LTD.,
Guildford, Surrey

*To Grantham's local historians of the past,
to whom we owe so much:
Edmund Turnor, the Rev. Benjamin Street, Sir Alfred Welby and
George Mitcham.*

List of Illustrations

Acknowledgements

It gives me great pleasure to acknowledge the willing assistance of Alan Leventhall and his staff at Grantham Library; and also the help of Lincolnshire County Council, without whose co-operation in allowing me to reproduce pictures in their collection at Grantham Library the book could not have been produced. I should also like to thank my friend, Michael Pointer, who earlier gave me my first chance to write for publication. Finally, thanks to my wife, Nita, and her trusty word processor for all the work they did together.

Illustration Acknowledgements

The following photographs are taken from the author's collection: nos. 10, 12, 14, 22-4, 36, 38, 62, 68, 85-7, 96-8, 105, 112-14, 117, 118, 126-34, 142, 145, 149-54. All others are held by Grantham Library.

List of known photographers whose work is included in this book:

C. Allen
W. Brooks
E. Burton
J. Cliffe
Emary of Grantham
Elliott & Fry
P. H. Faulkner
S. G. Gamble
Paul Girdlestone
Edwin Hadley

Howard & Jones
Walter Lee
F. R. Marshall
T. J. Norton
H. Platts
Henry Preston
J. Priest
G. Scothern
F. G. Simpson & Co.
Lino Tassi

Introduction

Grantham probably originated as a sixth-century Saxon settlement founded in a river valley on a well-drained layer of sand and gravel. The Saxon name is believed to mean 'the settlement on the gravel or sand bank', and all recent town centre developments have revealed a thick layer of sand lying 18-24 in. below street level. Present-day Welby Street was, in the 19th century, called Sandpit Lane.

When the Vikings invaded in the eighth and ninth centuries they found that the best lands had already been settled by the Saxons and, therefore, built their own dwellings in the less hospitable areas. On the hills surrounding Grantham are settlements such as Gonerby, Barrowby, Somerby and Harrowby, all ending with the Danish suffix -by, meaning farm. Grantham was situated in the heart of the Danelaw, very close to four of the five Danish boroughs: Lincoln, Stamford, Nottingham and Leicester. Derby, the fifth, is 40 miles away. By the ninth century Grantham seems to have been the capital of an important local estate and to have remained prosperous during the time of the Danish settlement.

At the time of the Norman Conquest the town belonged to Queen Edith, wife of Edward the Confessor and sister of King Harold. It remained a royal possession until 1696. We know from Domesday Book that by 1086 the population of the town and its soke (the land under its jurisdiction) was about one thousand three hundred. It had four water mills and a church. Mills continued to be worked on all four sites until the 19th century – at Slate Mill, Willoughby's, Spitalgate and Queen's (East Street, formerly Well Lane). The Saxon church probably stood on the site of St Wulfram's, which was founded *c.*1140.

The bridging of the River Trent at Newark in about 1168 increased Grantham's importance considerably by altering the main route from London to the north so that it ran through the town centre. Hitherto travellers had used Ermine Street, the Roman road which ran along the limestone ridge two miles to the east of Grantham.

Colonel Sir Alfred Welby (1849-1937), a well-known local historian, described early medieval Grantham as having

> ... miry tracks converging on the market-stead where the country folk exchanged their produce for the wares of the town at stalls licensed by the king as lord, or at small dark shops. A special place was set apart for the sale of fish, so necessary when fasting was generally observed ... some streets and alleys of small houses radiated from this centre of business, and beyond them lay the homesteads standing detached in the grassland. The church, on the same site as now, was an aisleless romanesque structure with a rectangular chancel and probably with a comparatively tall western bell-tower.

By the 13th century wool was the basis of Lincolnshire's economy, the area being famed for its long-wool sheep; Boston was the main wool-exporting port in the country. In Grantham the magnificent west front and 280-ft. tower and spire of St Wulfram's church bear witness to the prosperity brought by the wool trade. In 1280 the market place had to be moved to allow for the expansion of the church. It was resited between the Grey Friars' building and the *Angel Inn*, next to the main highway. The market cross was constructed shortly afterwards. In 1314 the Grey Friars brought fresh water to the town centre via a conduit, which was either repaired or replaced by the Borough Council in 1597. The 'new' conduit is still located on the west side of the Market Place.

Grantham was granted its Charter of Incorporation by Edward IV in 1463, probably as a reward for its support of the Yorkists during the Wars of the Roses. After the battle of Wakefield in 1460 the victorious Lancastrian army under Margaret of Anjou sacked and pillaged Grantham on its way south. A further charter was granted to the town in 1484 by Richard III – one of very few to be awarded by him. It licensed the borough to hold a Wednesday market and two annual fairs. The market lapsed in the 19th century, but Grantham still holds a mid-Lent fair, during which the relevant part of the charter is read from the steps of the 1280 market cross.

In 1541 Grantham, together with Lincoln, Grimsby and Stamford, was described as 'decayed'. Despite this, the King's School was endowed in 1528, and the original building in Church Street is still in use as the school library. Nearby, the late 14th-century Grantham House was extended in 1574. By 1633 the town had evidently regained much of its former prosperity: a tax demand for ship money from the borough and soke amounted to £159 compared to Stamford's £53 and Lincoln's £200.

The town suffered little damage during the Civil War, despite its proximity to the Royalist strongholds of Newark and Belvoir Castle. The Eleanor Cross, probably located on the present-day St Peter's Hill, was destroyed in 1644-5, and some tombs in St Wulfram's were damaged, many angels being defaced. Far more disastrous was a fire in 1663 which destroyed many buildings and caused thousands of pounds worth of damage. This is probably one reason why only four timbered buildings in the town are known to have survived.

In 1696 William III granted the manor to William Bentinck, Earl of Portland, and in the next year Celia Fiennes described Grantham as a 'well built town of stone'. Daniel Defoe also visited the town, describing it in the 1720s as follows:

> This is a neat, pleasant well-built and populous town, has a good market and the inhabitants are said to have a very good trade and are generally rich. There is also a very good free school here. This town lying on the Great North Road is famous as well as Stamford for abundance of good inns, some of them fit to entertain persons of the greatest quality and their retinue, and it is a great advantage to the place.

Roads in the town were little better than tracks, muddy in wet weather and dusty in dry. In 1706 a journey from London to York took four days 'if God permits'. The turnpike acts changed this state of affairs and toll gates were built on the roads to Foston (1725), Stamford (1739), Nottingham (1758), Melton Mowbray (1780), and Bridge End (1804). Macadam acted as consultant surveyor on the roads to Nottingham and Foston. The increased number of travellers resulting from the improved roads boosted trade. More inns were built, including the *George* in 1780 and the *Mail Inn*. The *Angel* was a medieval inn and over the centuries many members of the royal family enjoyed hospitality there en route between the capitals of England and Scotland. This inn was extended in 1776.

The Grantham-Nottingham canal opened in 1797, Grantham importing coal and exporting grain. Local carriers now worked the canals and the River Trent to Gainsborough, Nottingham and Shardlow (Derbyshire) every week. On the opening of the canal the *Stamford Mercury* of 10 May 1793 reported that 'an oxe of nearly 70 stone weight was roasted on the occasion and the populace were regaled with beef and ale in great abundance ... in the evening the town was beautifully illuminated'.

The 18th century saw many changes in Grantham. The Georgians built in red brick, replacing many of the stone buildings of earlier centuries. Despite the redevelopment of the 1950s and 1960s, Grantham still has many Georgian buildings, including Vine House

(1764) and the Rectory (1789). The first Dissenting chapel was built in Castlegate in 1729. The Guildhall was rebuilt in 1787, incorporating a sessions hall, rooms for council meetings and a prison. It was extended again in 1823 to include a treadmill and a larger prison which could house 30 prisoners. It was replaced by the present Guildhall on St Peter's Hill in 1867-9. A theatre, demolished in 1952, was built in Swinegate in 1800. More houses were built to accommodate the growing population; for example, the Little Gonerby development along North Parade.

The 19th century saw yet more change. At the beginning of the century the population was about three thousand; by 1901 it had grown to about nineteen thousand. The Grantham Extension Act of 1879 incorporated Little Gonerby, New Somerby, Earlesfield and Spitalgate, creating 'Greater Grantham'. Richard Hornsby's factory was situated at Spitalgate, and its success contributed much to the development of the town. It began as a blacksmithy in 1815, expanding into an engineering works with a workforce of 2,000 by the end of the century. Strikes at the factory were not unusual. In 1890, 1,400 men stopped work for seven weeks, which brought great hardship to local families. The churches, however, rallied round, and the factory owners provided dinner for over 1,000 children.

In 1850 the Ambergate, Nottingham and Boston Railway Company built a line from Grantham to Colwick, near Nottingham. The station was next to the canal basin and the line duplicated the route of the canal. In 1852 the Great Northern Railway connected Grantham with London, and eventually Edinburgh, via the main east coast line. The company bought out the smaller rival railway company and purchased the canal, which quickly became redundant. The Old Wharf was taken over by local coal merchants.

The present-day town centre at St Peter's Hill was known during the early 19th century as 'The Wilderness', but was tidied up when Sir Isaac Newton's statue was erected there in 1857. Newton was born in 1642 at Woolsthorpe-by-Colsterworth, six miles away, and was educated at Grantham Grammar School. The former Guildhall, in Guildhall Street, was replaced in the late 1860s by a new building, designed by William Watkins of Lincoln, situated behind the Newton statue.

Several churches were erected during the Victorian era, joining St Wulfram's whose tower and spire had dominated Grantham's skyline for centuries. St John's (1840-1) was known as a chapel until May 1844, when it became the parish church of Spitalgate. In Little Gonerby, St Mary's Catholic church was built in 1831-2, and St Saviour's was consecrated in 1880.

Bridges were built over the River Witham, opening up large areas of land to the east of the town where many Victorian mansions were built. Most have now been converted for non-residential use. Stonebridge House is the police station, and Elsham House is part of Grantham College of Further Education. The Barracks on Sandon Road were erected in 1851 and extended in 1872, the public baths on Wharf Road were built in 1854, and the Salvation Army Citadel on London Road in 1896. The cemetery on Harrowby Road opened on 1 May 1857, and Grantham's third and last work-house, on Dysart Road, in June 1892.

Gas first became available in October 1833, and tap water in 1850. The sewage works at the Corporation farm at Marston were in use from 1881 onwards. Improvements in medicine and hygiene led to the establishment in 1849-50 of a dispensary in Finkin Street. Even so, 28 per cent of all burials at St Wulfram's church between 1875 and 1894 were of babies aged two years and under, and seven and a half per cent were aged between two and five years.

The Victorians were great founders of societies, though some existed much earlier, for example the St Wulfram's Society of Change Ringers which dates from 1781. The Grantham Philosophical Institution, established in 1837, held its meetings in the spacious hall in Finkin Street, next door to the Methodist church. The main room was octagonal, with a library below and a museum above. In 1847 a Public Literary Institution was established for the purpose of providing 'Instruction, a Library Reading Room, Lectures etc. for the Industrious classes' for a small annual charge. The Exchange Hall (one of two corn exchanges, both built in 1852) provided space for lectures, and by 1872 had a library of more than 2,500 books. The Grantham Photographic Society and the Amateur Art Society were both founded in 1881, and the football and bowls clubs in 1876.

Many street names contain the word 'blue' as a result of a feud in 1802 between two important local families, the Manners from Belvoir Castle and the Brownlows from Belton House. Grantham was notorious as a 'pocket borough' and traditionally each family sent one M.P. to parliament. In 1802, however, Sir William Manners decided to send two candidates and, to emphasise his power, renamed much of his property. The *King's Arms* became the *Blue Ram*, the *White Horse* became the *Blue Horse*, the *Green Man* became the *Blue Man*, and property was built at Blue Court and Bluegate.

Within days of the outbreak of World War One on 4 August 1914, the construction of Belton Camp commenced. Eventually this camp, together with nearby Harrowby Camp, would house up to 25,000 soldiers, at a time when the civilian population of Grantham was only 19,000, giving great impetus to trade in the town. In September 1914 a Newark correspondent complained, 'Newark hasn't got a range, nor a Belton Park, nor a Lord Brownlow, nor any enterprise. There is a good deal more trade in Grantham now than when the war started.' Tea houses and cafés thrived in the town, as well as crime and prostitution; as a result, Grantham was the first town in England to have a policewoman. Many street names are associated with the camps, including Signal Road and Range Road. Hill Avenue was named after General Henry Cecil de la Montague Hill, who founded the Machine Gun Corps in Belton Park in 1915. This was later nicknamed the 'suicide club', a third of its members becoming war casualties. Its standard is now in St Wulfram's church. Approximately 800 Grantham men were killed during the war. The official memorial was unveiled in 1920 and Wyndham Park was opened in July 1924. It was named after Captain the Hon. W. R. Wyndham, who was killed near Ypres in November 1914.

The inter-war years brought more problems to Grantham. In 1922, 49 per cent of the working population was unemployed and the town was classed as a distressed area. Ruston & Hornsby Ltd. (formerly Richard Hornsby & Sons Ltd.) had lost their overseas markets as a result of the war. Aveling-Barford, however, came to Grantham in 1934, taking over part of Ruston & Hornsby's works. This firm prospered until the 1980s. A council estate, Walton Gardens, was built for the company's key workers who had moved to Grantham from Rochester (the Aveling connection) and Peterborough (Barford). The firm quickly became the town's main employer, with a workforce of well over 2,000 by the 1950s. In 1937 Grantham's fortunes received another boost when R. H. Neal, a firm of Ealing crane manufacturers, established itself in the former factory of A. C. Potter & Co. on Dysart Road.

World War Two brought much work. The larger factories received government contracts, and the British Manufacturing and Research Company was set up specifically as a munitions factory. In addition, a Ministry of Aircraft Production factory was established on Springfield Road. Until the blitz Grantham was the most bombed town in England after Canterbury, excluding London. This was probably because of the amount of war work being carried out there. During the war Grantham suffered 386 alerts, compared with nearby Nottingham's 223; almost three thousand properties were damaged, nearly a hundred people killed and almost two hundred injured. Almost as many Grantham civilians were killed as were Grantham men in the armed forces.

Although the population of the town expanded during this time, the increase was not as marked as during the First World War. R.A.F. Spitalgate was part of Flying Training Command, and for some time No. 5 Group Bomber Command had its headquarters at St Vincent's, where the 'Dam Busters' raid was organised. The R.A.F. Regiment was later founded in Alma Park. In 1943 the American forces arrived and, on 17 September 1944, American transport aircraft, C47 Skytrains (Dakotas), pulled their gliders over Grantham en route for Arnhem. Many British paratroopers were stationed in the large country houses around Grantham and remembrance services are still held for them in several local villages.

After the war the need for reconstruction throughout Britain and Europe kept local factories very busy until the recession of the 1970s. Ruston & Hornsby had already closed down in 1963. The introduction of diesel-powered engines in the 1960s, together with 'Beeching's axe', was responsible for the loss of many jobs connected with the railway. Nevertheless, although Grantham is 106 miles from London, the introduction of the high-speed train has made it a commuter town, several hundred residents travelling to and from King's Cross each working day.

In 1974 local government reorganisation took away the town's borough status. Also, the face of the town has altered very much in recent years, especially in the High Street, and one side of Watergate has been changed beyond recognition. Many Georgian buildings have disappeared and the Grantham Civic Trust, founded in 1961, is still fighting to preserve the character of the town.

Bibliography

Allen, Jim, *The Grantham Connection* (1986).
Bond, Lawrence, and Knapp, Malcolm G., *Georgian Houses in Grantham* (1987).
Bowen, R. and Willard, C. P., *The Story of Grantham and its Countryside* (1949).
Branson, S. J., *The King's School, Grantham* (1988).
Honeybone, Michael, *The Book of Grantham* (1980).
Kelly's Directory.
Knapp, Malcolm G., *Grantham Walkabout* (1981).
Pevsner, Nikolaus, and Harris, John, *The Buildings of England – Lincolnshire*, revised by Nicholas Antram, 2nd edn. (1989).
Pointer, Michael, *Hornsby's of Grantham 1815-1918* (1976).
Pointer, Michael, *The Glory of Grantham* (1978).
The Grantham Red Book (1894 and 1902).
Turnor, Edmund, *History of the Town and Soke of Grantham* (1806).
White's Directory.

Churches

1. A fine view of St Wulfram's church tower and spire from the south-west. It is impossible to photograph this scene now as many mature trees obscure the view.

2. A quiet part of old Grantham, showing the west front of St Wulfram's. The 18th- and 19th-century houses on the left are part of Church Trees, known as Church Pavement in the 19th century.

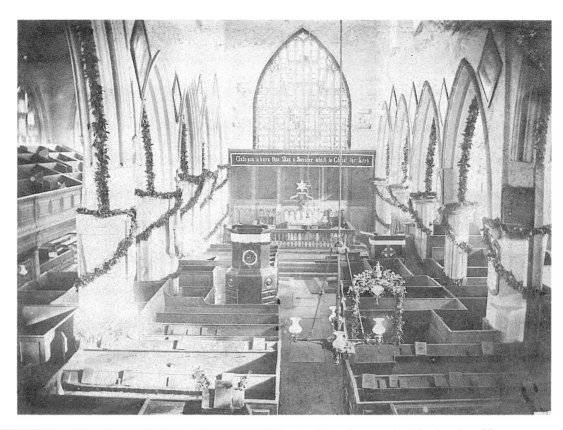

3. This photograph of the interior of St Wulfram's was taken *c*.1860 before the restoration by Sir Gilbert Scott. It shows the boxed pews, the gallery on the left and the high pulpit built in 1792.

4. The interior of St Wulfram's in 1880-1, after the great alterations.

5. By 1883 a larger reredos had been installed, partially blocking the east window. It was dedicated by Canon Body on 27 May 1883.

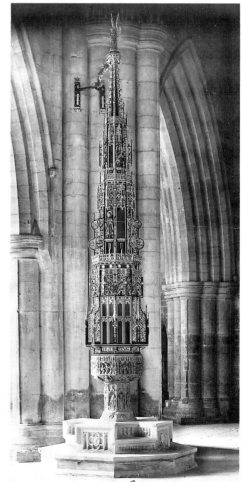

6. The late 15th-century font with its Victorian cover. It is 26 ft. high and made of oak.

7. Harvest festival at the Finkin Street Methodist church which was built in 1840, replacing an earlier church.

8. St Saviour's mission church, Easter 1883. Mr. Charles Chambers (after whom Chambers Street was named) gave the site for this church in Manners Street, and in May 1880 the foundation stone was laid by Lady Brownlow. The church closed in the late 1940s.

9. St Mary's Roman Catholic church on North Parade was built in 1831 and opened by Bishop Walsh of Nottingham on 1 May 1832. The church was completely remodelled in 1884 and 1966. This photograph was taken before 1884.

10. St John's church, Spitalgate, between the years 1841-83. It was consecrated by the Rt. Rev. John Kaye, Bishop of Lincoln, on 2 November 1841, and during 1883-4 extensive alterations were carried out. These included the building of a new chancel, extensions to the nave and new seats for the entire church. Mr. James Hornsby generously provided a quarter of the cost.

11. St John's church was built during 1840-1. This photograph shows the all-male choir on an outing in the 1880s.

12. St Anne's iron church was opened on 3 January 1884 by the Bishop of Lincoln and was locally called the 'tin tabernacle'. It was built to serve the expanding area of the town known as 'New Somerby' or 'Harrowby Within'. It was replaced by the present St Anne's church.

13. In 1946 the bells of St Wulfram's were recast. This photograph shows members of the church, including Canon Leeke and Lawrence Bond, with the verger, Mr. George Pacey (on the right). The party also included bell-ringer Mr. Tom Relf, keeping an eye on the tenor bell at the foundry of John Taylor & Co. of Loughborough.

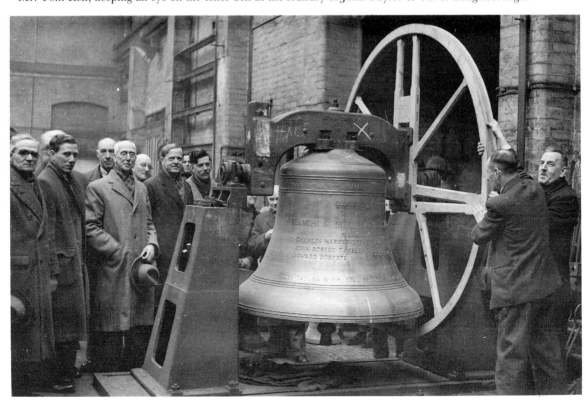

Industry and Commerce

14. Grantham was represented at this agricultural show around the 1890s. James Coultas machinery, all apparently sold, stands in the foreground, and Hornsby traction engines are in the far distance. During the Great War, Richard Hornsby & Co. lost its overseas market and after the war amalgamated with another firm to become Ruston & Hornsby, with its head office at Lincoln. The Depression hit Grantham badly, but in 1934 some of Ruston & Hornsby's surplus factory space was taken over by Aveling-Barford Ltd., makers of road rollers and earth-moving equipment.

The Journal of the Royal Agricultural Society of England,
No. xxvii, Second Series, Vol. xix, Part II. 1883.

REPORT OF IMPLEMENTS AT YORK, BY JOHN COLEMAN, ESQ.

Judges—T. P. Outhwaite, Esq.; George Gibbons, Esq.; and John Coleman, Esq.

FIG. 29--J. P. COULTAS' CHIMNEY ELEVATOR.

J.P. COULTAS' PATENT.

"MR. JAMES COULTAS, of Grantham, exhibited a Patent Apparatus by means of which the Chimneys of Portable Engines can be raised or lowered with great ease. To show the utility of this novelty it is only necessary to remind our readers, that hitherto, when this operation has to be performed the attendant must get on the engine. The chimney is often very hot, and it is not an easy job either to raise or lower. It is farther possible that an accident might occur during the operation, and there is the continual risk of damage to the working parts of the Engine by the carelessness of the attendant. Securely fastened to the smoke-box is an endless screw, worked by a handle, which actuates a small windlass, and thereby winds up the chimney by means of a chain which passes through an eye in a plate at the bottom of the chimney, and is attached to a rod which terminates at the top of the chimney. The advantages claimed by the Patentee are—the great saving of time; prevention of accidents; no risk of damage to the working rods and other parts of the Engine by the attendant standing on them; no bolts required for holding chimney up."

				£	s	d
The cost of the Apparatus complete for 8-h.p.			...	£3	10	0
Ditto	ditto	ditto	for 10 & 12-h.p.	4	17	6

This Apparatus can be fixed to any existing Portable Engines, new or old.

APPARATUS OR LICENSE MAY BE OBTAINED FROM

Jas. COULTAS, or the Patentee, Perseverance Iron Works, Grantham.

15. James Coultas was a successful local firm, though it never rivalled Hornsby's in size. This chimney elevator would have been a useful adjunct to a Hornsby portable engine. The Perseverance Iron Works on Station Road is now the railway station car park.

16. Malting was an important industry in Grantham in the 19th century, over a dozen maltsters being listed in the 1872 *White's Directory*. This turn-of-the-century photograph shows Lee and Grinling's workforce outside No. 12 Malting on Bridge End Road. The large wooden tools were used to prevent the grain from being bruised or broken. The man with the beard was Mr. Berridge, the foreman.

17.   The Grantham Dairy Co. of 85 Westgate showing off their first prize display at the turn of the century. The 'first class dining room upstairs' catered for cyclists and other parties. Notice the cobbled street of Westgate. The cobbles are now hidden under layers of tarmac.

18. W. B. Harrison & Sons of 17-18 Watergate show off their wicker and cane furniture at an exhibition in Tabernacle Street, London. In 1896 the firm was described as a 'wholesale and export manufacturer of children's carriages and mail carts, wicker bath chairs, japanners, bamboo fancy articles of all descriptions and willow merchant'. Harrison's factory was at the rear of the shop.

19. Horse sales used to be held on the first Wednesday of each month. This photograph, taken from the railway embankment, shows a sale at the turn of the century, not long after the Cattle Market had opened.

20. The Cattle Market from Dysart Road. The photograph can be dated to 1903 by one of the Theatre Royal advertisements. These advertisements are a superb record of early 20th-century Grantham commerce. Messrs. Escritt & Barrell are still successful auctioneers in the town.

21. C. W. Dixon's, the complete house furnisher, of 67 Wharf Road. This photograph shows a pre-1914 display in the upstairs showroom.

22. The 'Shorturn Tractor
Plough' of 1928, produced by
Ruston & Hornsby. The driver was
Mr. Tommy Roberts.

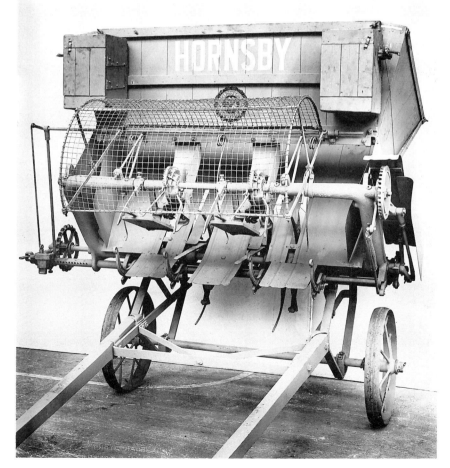

23. A Ruston & Hornsby Steam
Trusser of 1928.

24. R. H. Neal, crane makers, took over the disused factory of A. C. Potter & Co. in Dysart Road in 1937. This photograph shows various types of crane being built in the rather cramped assembly shop. Grantham's crane building industry continued until Coles Cranes closed down in 1984.

25.   Vacu-lug started in a large shed at Great Ponton. The firm was so successful that it moved to much bigger premises in Gonerby Hill Foot.

26.   An aerial view of industrial Grantham, 19 July 1957, looking towards the south-west with Ruston & Hornsby's in the foreground. Most has now disappeared.

Sport and Recreation

27. A Grantham ladies' tennis team photographed by F. G. Simpson in late Victorian times.

28. A fancy dress parade, with the leaders assembled on the Guildhall steps. Such events took place regularly on Bank Holiday Mondays. The parades ended on the London Road sports ground where the fancy dress costumes were judged and races took place.

29. Children and dogs enjoying a paddle in the River Witham in what, after the First World War, became Wyndham Park.

30. A ladies' football team from Hornsby's factory, which played in a charity match against a team of men with their hands tied behind their backs. The match took place on the Harlaxton Road ground, probably in 1916. The proceeds were given to provide comforts for men in the hospital at the Barracks. The lady on the left with the fox fur is the referee, Mrs. Ethel Huthwaite.

31. A proud moment in the life of Grantham Avenue Football Club in the 1905-6 season when the reserve side won both the Minor Cup and the Grantham and District League.

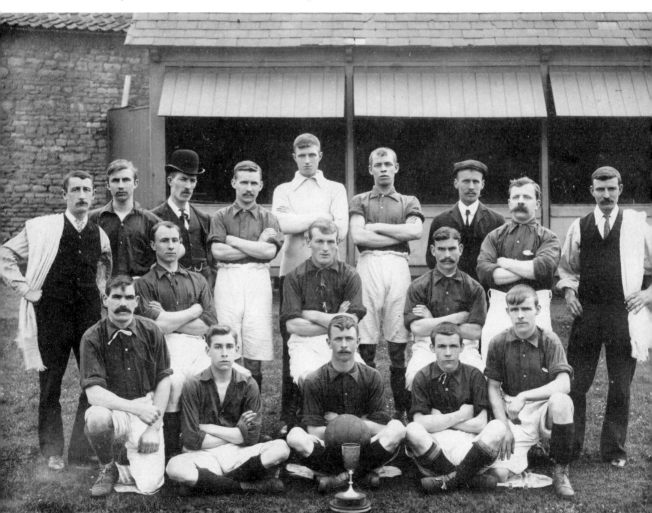

32. An end of season photograph of Grantham Avenue Football Club, 1911-12.

33.   The New Somerby Cricket Club, *c.*1905, on what appears to be the London Road ground. Some of the men seem to have played in collar and tie.

34. How times have changed! This photograph by Emary of London Road shows the Middlemore Glee Singers made up ready for the then very popular 'Nigger Minstrel Show'.

GRANTHAM
STEEPLE CHASE,

Thursday, March 29, 1838.

A SWEEPSTAKES of Five Guineas each, with **Fifty Guineas** added; the Last Horse to pay the Second Horse's Stake. Four-year old, 11st. 3lbs.; five, 11st. 10lbs; six, 12st. 3lbs. Mares and Geldings allowed 3lbs. All disputes to be settled by the Stewards, or whom they may appoint. The riders to weigh at the George Inn at Twelve o'Clock, and proceed to the ground at One. Subscriptions will be received by Mr. Ridge.

Mr. Skipworth's br. h. King Cole, aged ....*Blue and White and Black Cap*
—Patchett's ch. h. Grasshopper, aged ....*Blue and Black Cap*
—Whitworth's b. h. Gamester, aged ....*Crimson and White*
—Walker's br. h. Highlander, late Antelope, aged, *Blue & White Sleeves & Black Cap*
—Ditto's br. h. Caledonian, late Fisherman, six years old..............*Plaid*
—Wallis' gr. h. Valentine, aged ....*Yellow and Black Cap*
—Green's ch. h. Corringham, aged
—Burbidge's b. h. Cannon Ball, aged ....*Blue and White*
—Whitworth's br. h. Nathan, aged ....*Crimson and Black Cap*
—Brook's br. m. Madam, aged.....................*Purple and Crimson Cap*
—Green's b. h. Radical, six years old..........*Pink and White and Black Cap*
—Butler's ch. h. Stranger, six years old ....*Blue*

No person will be allowed to ride on the ground except those engaged in the Race.

RIDGE, PRINTER, GRANTHAM.

35. Grantham steeplechase, 1838. The race course was in the Somerby Hill area.

36.   Dysart Park baths in 1936. These are now closed, as are the Wyndham Park baths at the other end of the town.

37.   The 7th Grantham Scouts' garden fête at 'Norman Leys', June 1955.

38. The Grantham town band under the direction of Mr. Henry Charles (Harry) Sale, photographed inside the Barracks, *c*.1938. Mr. George Pacey, St Wulfram's church verger, is seen here as drum major (middle of back row). Originally the Ruston & Hornsby band, it is now known as the Grantham Concert Band.

Buildings

39.   The Guildhall on St Peter's Hill is a marvellous example of a mid-19th-century building, completed early in 1870. This is how it looked in April 1955 before the top was altered. This building replaced an 18th-century Guildhall on the High Street at the corner of Guildhall Street.

40. A fine painting of 1832 reproduced many years later by G. Scoffin of Chapel Street. It shows the *Angel Inn* on the High Street and also the galleried house next door. This was demolished in 1897 to make way for a new building for Boot's, the cash chemists.

41. Grantham's medieval inn changed its name from the *Angel* to the *Angel and Royal Hotel* after a visit by H.R.H. The Prince of Wales in 1866. The hotel name even appears on the ornate lamp posts, and stables can be seen in the distance through the archway.

42. W. B. Harrison's premises at the bottom of Watergate. The site has been totally changed and none of the buildings in this photograph have survived.

43. The Earlesfield tanneries were situated off Harlaxton Road and by the side of the Grantham-Nottingham canal, from which they drew their water. The business was carried on by Messrs. A. & J. Shaw & Sons Ltd., and their name is now commemorated by a road name in the Earlesfield district. This photograph was taken c.1912. The company went bankrupt around 1920.

44. Demolition of the old granary at the wharf of the Grantham-Nottingham canal in October 1929. The canal flowed underneath the arch.

45. The *Crown and Anchor* in Swinegate in 1937. The building has gone, the area has been cleared and the King's Court nursing home now occupies the site.

46. The 'Noah's Ark', *c.*1880, on High Street between the *Angel and Royal Hotel* and the *Cross Swords* public house. Notice the ark between the windows, above the proprietor's name.

47. The *Sun Inn* on the corner of Brownlow Street and Broad Street. This was demolished in 1964 and was eventually replaced by Premier Court.

48. The *Granby Inn* (*right*) and the *Blue Lion* (*left*). The *Granby* is still a public house today but the *Blue Lion* premises have now been converted into offices. The old Butter Market Hall, later used as a store for market stalls, is next to the telephone box.

49. The entrance from Broad Street into Vere Court. The house on the right, with its typical Grantham moustachioed window lintels, has survived but the house on the left has been demolished to make way for the Premier Restaurant car park.

50. Vere Court looking south towards Vere Street. In the far distance the bottom of Watergate can be seen.

51. & 52. Typical 19th-century working-class housing developments – 'yards, courts and places' hidden behind the main streets. These two photographs show Millards Place (*above*) and Millards Yard (*below*).

53. The rear of Nos. 14 to 22 Charles Street in 1934. This street, located behind North Parade, is much changed today.

54. Union Court, Inner Street, under demolition in the mid-1930s. Note the Ruston & Hornsby chimneys in the background.

55. Bourne Cottages, Inner Street, were demolished in 1934.

56. Welby Street, formerly Sand Pit Lane, also had 'yards, courts and places'. In 1927 it comprised Caborns Yard, Bradleys Yard, Sellors Yard, Greenwoods Row, Welby Row, Souths Yard, Garden Cottages, Banfields Yard and Newhams Yard. This photograph is of Vine Place, part of Welby Row in Welby Street.

57. The privies and wash-houses of Greenwoods Row.

58. Drawing by John Buckler (1770-1851) of an old building thought to have been in the High Street backing on to Butchers Row. A fine piece of 12th- or 13th-century work, perhaps from this ancient chapel, was destroyed in the cellar of No. 21 Market Place in the late 1880s.

59. View of the inside of the chapel (looking east).

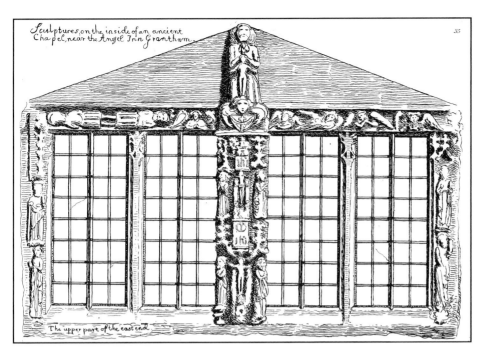

Sculptures, on the inside of an ancient Chapel, near the Angel Inn Grantham.

35

The upper part of the east end

60. Sculptures inside the chapel.

The north side.

Pub.ᵈ as the act directs, by I. Carter, Hamilton sᵗ Hyde Park Corner. May 1ˢᵗ 1791.

61. The north side of the chapel. Plates 59-61 were first published in May 1791.

62. The east side of High Street had many fine Georgian and Victorian buildings until the great property redevelopment boom of the late 1950s and early 1960s. One of the many casualties was the *Red Lion Hotel* which closed in 1961.

Railways

THE
GRANTHAM JOURNAL
Of Useful, Instructive, & Entertaining Knowledge;
AND MONTHLY ADVERTISER.

PUBLISHED ON THE FIRST DAY OF EACH MONTH BY JOHN ROGERS AND SON, WALKERGATE, GRANTHAM.

No. 3.]   APRIL, 1854.   [ONE PENNY.

MONTHLY CIRCULATION
OF
THE GRANTHAM JOURNAL
1,150.

The columns of the JOURNAL are open to the correspondence of all parties *free of expense*; the Publishers reserving to themselves the right of rejecting unsuitable communications.

Marriages and Deaths will also be inserted *without charge*.

For the accommodation of those parties who have expressed a wish to send *The Grantham Journal* to their friends in America, Australia, and other places, an edition of four pages will be issued, which will contain all the News, Marriages, Deaths, Correspondence, and Advertisements.

COPIES FOR SENDING BY POST, must be ordered three days prior to the time of publication, as only the required number will be printed.

THE NEW CRYSTAL PALACE, SYDENHAM.
TO BE OPENED BY HER MAJESTY, ABOUT MAY 24.

In a future number we shall give a large and splendid exterior view of the Palace, as it will appear on the opening day.

THE attention of all requiring and giving employment of any kind is respectfully invited to Proposals for Establishing in Grantham, on a different principle from any other hitherto attempted, a

REGISTER OFFICE FOR SERVANTS,
AND ALSO FOR EVERY DESCRIPTION OF PERSONS IN QUEST OF EMPLOYMENT.

The Repeal of the Duty on Advertisements has induced this attempt, to supply a want which we believe has been long felt in this Town and Neighbourhood.

The advantages of this Office over others, consists in the publicity that will be given to it by

THE ADVERTISEMENT
OF EVERY APPLICATION.

THE REGISTRATION
Together with the ADVERTISEMENT, if not more than *three lines*, will cost the Parties wanting Situations

NINE PENCE
Including any trouble that may attend the taking down of particulars and answering personal applicants. The same thing may be done per post, when an answer will be returned for THREE PENCE more, enclosed in Postage Stamps. All Parties must be prepared to give satisfactory References.

EMPLOYERS
Requiring Hands, Domestic or other Servants, or Labourers, will also have *Registration* made of their wants, together with

AN ADVERTISEMENT,
If not more than four Lines, In the *Grantham Journal* for ONE SHILLING, and every effort will be made to supply their wants.

Established by
J. ROGERS AND SON,
JOURNAL OFFICE, WALKERGATE, GRANTHAM.

PAGE WOODCOCK'S
WIND PILLS
CANNOT BE EQUALLED AS A FAMILY MEDICINE.

FIFTY THOUSAND BOXES
Of these Pills have been sold within the short space of a few months, and the Sale is rapidly increasing!

The *surprising efficacy* of these Pills in all derangements of the *Stomach, Bowels, and Liver*, is truly wonderful! They are especially recommended for the following Complaints: WIND in the STOMACH and BOWELS, INDIGESTION, Spasms, Costiveness, Giddiness and Sick Head-ache, Heartburn, Disturbed sleep, Palpitation of the Heart, Colic.

Great Northern Time Tables.

SUNDAYS.—Leaves Grantham for York 12 45 a. m. *Parl.*—and 11 41 p. m. *first and second.*—Leaves for London 6 50 a. m. *first and second.*—2 10 p. m. *first, second, third.* and 12 0 p. m. *first and second class.*
SLEAFORD.—An Omnibus leaves Grantham on week days at 8 45 afternoon.—Leaves *Sleaford* at 8.35 morning.

Amergate.—Grantham & Nottingham.

NATIONAL PROVINCIAL LIFE & FIRE INSURANCE OFFICES,
127, CHEAPSIDE, LONDON.
TRUSTEES.

LIFE SOCIETY. GUARANTEE FUND—FIFTY THOUSAND POUNDS.

The peculiar and distinctive features of this Society consist—

I. In allowing no member, when unable to continue his payments, to lose the benefit of the sums which he has paid. For example:—Suppose a person aged thirty assured his life for £500, and at the end of seven years he found he was unable to keep up any further payments, in other Offices he would lose all he had paid in but in this Society he would be entitled to claim a FREE POLICY for £80 without any further payment or charge whatever.
This just and equitable principle must recommend itself to every one about to Assure.

II. Suppose also that this person, after having paid three years' premiums, was, through temporary losses or unforeseen circumstances, unable to meet his payment, and entertaining a hope that the following year he might be placed in a better position, and not being desirous of discontinuing the Assurance for £500, he would be allowed at any time to charge his Policy with the amount of the premium at £5 per cent. interest, either to be deducted from the £500 at his death, or the Policy may be freed at any time by his paying the amount due.

III. By making every Policy *Indisputable*, except in cases of Fraud, thereby rendering them negotiable instruments as security and entailing no trouble or inconvenience to the survivors.

IV. By making the Policies *payable to the Holder*, by which means a Policy may, by simple endorsement, and without the usual trouble and expense of assignment, be negotiated with the same facility as Bills of Exchange.
Thus it will be observed, that by the peculiar privileges and facilities allowed to the Policy Holders of this Society Policies become marketable like any other description of property.

The Society is established on the just principle of Mutual Life Assurance, returning to the Assured, by way of Bonus, the surplus above the cost price of the Assurance.

The justice and liberality of the principles of this Society, and their suitability to the wants of the public, have obtained for it the approbation and recommendation of the leading and influential Public Journals.

Progress of the Society.
The Directors desire to call attention to the following statement, showing the rapid increase of Business as compared with the last year, which they believe to be the best evidence of the growing appreciation on the part of the public of the advantages of Life Assurance, and of their confidence in the constitution and management of this Society.

NEW BUSINESS.	Amount of New Assurances completed.	Annual Income therefrom.
Year ending July, 1853	£183,007	£6,141 7 9
Year ending July, 1852	123,860	4,198 5 10
Excess of the past Year over the corresponding previous year	£59,147	£1,943 1 11

Examples of the Beneficial Effects of Life Assurance.
Cases taken from the Books of the Society.

No. of Policy.	Name.	Agency.	Date of First Payment.	Date of Claim.	Length of time Assured.	Sums paid for Premiums.	Sums paid to Representatives.
241	G. H.	Rochdale	Dec. 8, 1851	Mar. 12, 1853	1¼ year	£6 15 6	£300
372	G. T.	Bristol	May 20, 1852	Mar. 28, 1853	10 mths.	24 8 9	300
1848	W. R.	Newcastle	Jan. 26, 1853	July 6, 1853	6 mths.	12 40 4	400
746	T. P.	London	May 26, 1852	August 1853	1¼ year	19 8 5	300
1896	S. H.	Reading	Feb. 10, 1853	August 1853	6 mths.	3 3 11	250

64. A group of engine cleaners, *c.*1890. The loco shed in the background was demolished in 1960. The engine, No. 14, is a Stirling 2-2-2 single with 7 ft. 7 in. diameter driving wheels.

65. Grantham main line platforms before the 1923 reorganisation. The passenger bridge over the lines was replaced in February 1986.

66. Little change is discernible in this photograph taken 40 years later, in September 1963.

67. The station had five platforms in 1962, when this photograph was taken, but Platform One was soon to disappear and the others were then renumbered.

68. A Great Northern engine pulling a load of Hornsby agricultural equipment. The location is to the south of Springfield Road, near to the South Parade works. The tower of St John's church can be seen towards the left.

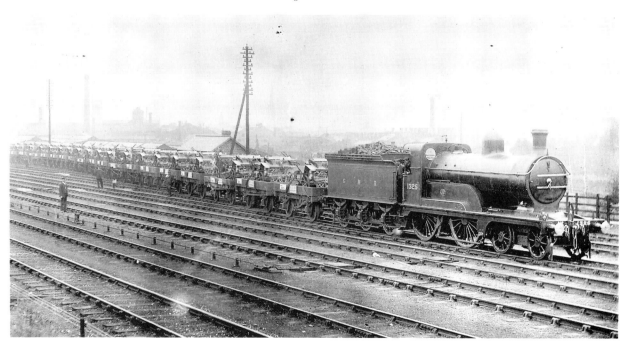

69. A G.N.R. express passing the Belton signal box which was closed in May 1922.

70. Grantham loco yard photographed on 6 September 1963, the day before its closure.

71. A local diesel train, probably from Boston or Skegness, pulls into Grantham station, passing the Grantham North signal box which has since been demolished.

72. Grantham's first station, photographed in 1951. This served the Grantham to Nottingham line for two years before the Great Northern main line opened in 1852. The station was situated between Old Wharf Road and Dysart Road.

73. The local coal merchants had their own trucks in which coal was delivered to the wharf direct from the pit. These two trucks and a horse and cart all belonged to Henry Bowman & Co. of the Great Northern Wharf.

Military Grantham

74. A contingent of the Sherwood Rangers (North Notts. Hussars) entering High Street after a thanksgiving service held at St Wulfram's church for the safe return of their comrades from the Boer War in 1901. Later, a banquet was held at the *George Hotel* in honour of the Grantham & District Active Service Squadron of the Sherwood Rangers.

75. Before the Territorial Army was
founded by Lord Haldane in April 1908,
after the Territorial and Reserve Forces Act
of 1907, many areas had their 'volunteers'.
This is the band of the Grantham
Volunteers, c.1900.

76. Long before World War One, Belton Park was used by the army. This photograph shows the Red Cross Cycle Corps, with not a bicycle in sight, at camp in the park well before the outbreak of the 'war to end all wars'.

77.   Photographed in August/September 1914 in Belton Park, this appears to be a medical inspection.

78.   The outbreak of the Great War brought a never-ending stream of wounded soldiers. These men, all volunteers, were the Grantham Red Cross team who met the trains bringing the wounded to Grantham station. They then took them to the Barracks wartime hospital.

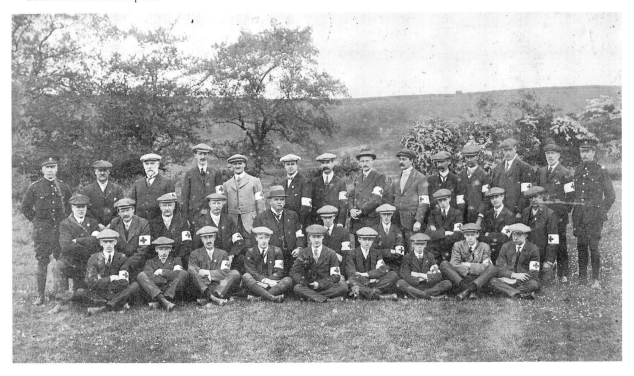

79. Local schoolboys of the King's School Officers' Training Corps in 1915. One wonders how many of the senior boys joined the army and survived the war.

80. Belton Park on the outskirts of the town quickly became a vast army training camp. Initially it was tented but very quickly the tents were replaced by wooden or corrugated iron huts.

81. Huts at Belton, near Belmont Tower.

82. The camp had its own railway system which was connected to the main Great Northern line near Manthorpe. Here, however, two Midland Railway trucks are in use.

11TH DIVISION LEAVES GRANTHAM. 1915.

83.   The 11th Division, including the 6th Battalion, Lincolnshire Regiment, trained at Belton Park, marches along Westgate on 5 April 1915. These smiling, fit young men little understood the horrors awaiting them in Gallipoli.

84.   A group of walking wounded with the nursing staff of Grantham military hospital at the Barracks on Sandon Road.

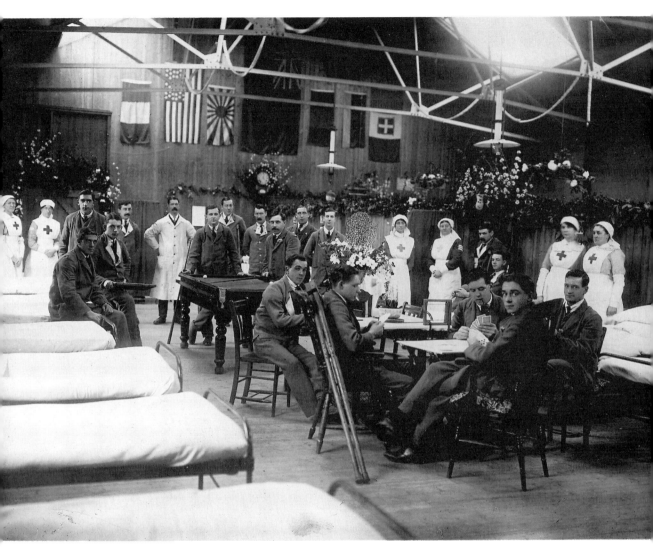

85. Christmas celebrations at the military hospital at Grantham Barracks in 1918.

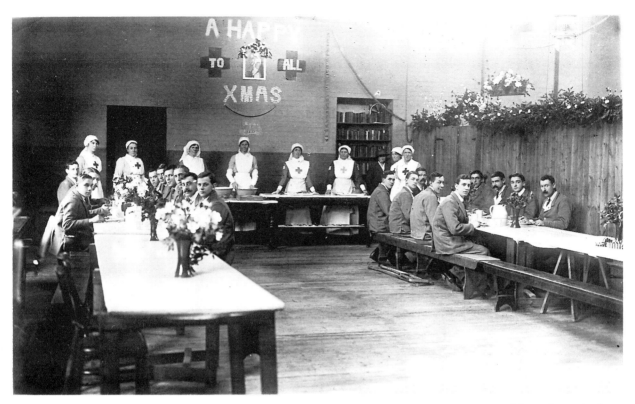

86. The war was over but the injuries remained. No doubt both staff and wounded servicemen were able to relax and enjoy the first peaceful Christmas in five years.

87. The 19th-century Barracks on Sandon Road with Great War guns outside. These made marvellous playthings for small boys until taken away for scrap.

People

88.   Grantham's fire engine and crew, including a lady water carrier, 1878. Sidney Gompertz Gamble was the photographer; he was also the local architect, surveyor and sanitary engineer, borough surveyor and treasurer. In 1892 he was appointed second officer of the Metropolitan fire brigade.

89. Zachariah Godfrey of Church Trees was the parish clerk, registrar of births and deaths, and vaccination officer for the Grantham Union District. He is seen here standing outside the west door of St Wulfram's church, probably at the time of his retirement from the office of parish clerk in 1884, a position he had held for 30 years.

90. William Brewster Harrison in his mayoral robes in 1895. He was a prominent businessman of the town.

91. An outing along the Grantham canal, apparently organised by the Salvation Army.

92. Frederick James Tollemache was M.P. for Grantham for many years, his political connection with the borough dating back to 1826. He died in 1888 and this statue was erected in 1891. It was unveiled in 1892 by Sir Hugh Cholmeley, Bart. This photograph was taken in November 1897 – Tollemache had just been 'elected' mayor, as the Borough Council could not agree who to choose.

93. Lord Brownlow and Capt. B. C. Thompson inspecting the Guard of Honour on the occasion of the granting of the Freedom of the Borough to Lord Brownlow in 1912.

94. Lord and Lady Brownlow on the steps of the Guildhall with the mayor of Grantham, J. W. Hornsby, during the same ceremony.

95.   Lord and Lady Brownlow with Lord Kitchener at Belton House in October 1914. Major General Hammersley who commanded the ill-fated 11th Division, then in training at Belton Park, is standing on Lord Kitchener's left.

96. Chief Constable John Casburn sits impressively in the middle of the front row of Grantham's special constables during the Great War. Grantham's first policewoman, Mrs. Edith Smith, can just be seen in the middle behind the back row.

97. Five nurses at the Barracks hospital during the Great War.

98. One of the many hundreds of locally taken photographs of wounded soldiers recovering from their injuries at the Barracks hospital. This photograph is of Private G. F. Burton, 2nd Battalion, Lincolnshire Regiment, whose left leg and hand were blown off by a 'whizz-bang' on the first day of the Battle of the Somme, 1 July 1916.

99.   Grantham suffered very badly during the Depression. Here the Duke of Kent is visiting the Grantham Occupation Centre in the Market Place. The duke had another Grantham connection – when his aircraft crashed in Scotland in 1942, one of the crew was Flight Sergeant E. J. Hewerdine of Grantham, now buried in the Harrowby Road cemetery.

100.   Henry Preston and his wife, Fanny, being met at Stoke Rochford Hall on the occasion of the Lincolnshire Naturalists' Union Field Meeting in June 1936.

101. The first borough librarian and museum curator was Walter George Summers, photographed *c*.1939. He expanded Henry Preston's original collection and built up the local history library. He retired in 1941.

102. Percy Willard came to Grantham as librarian in 1941 on a salary of £300 per annum plus war bonus! He continued to expand the museum and the local history collection. Mr. Willard was greatly missed when he left the local library in 1966 and went to the Stoke Rochford Teachers' Training College.

103.   Walter Lee, the great Grantham photographer, also had a consuming interest in drawing and painting. He formed the Grantham Art Club which met weekly in his studio from 1921-35 and which continued to flourish until shortly after the end of the Second World War. Walter Lee is second from the right in this photograph, probably taken in the early 1930s. A list on the back of the photograph names the following people who appear with Mr. Lee: Mr. D. B. Warren (a founder member of the Club), Mr. G. R. Scoffin, Mrs. Kirlew (teacher at K.G.G.S.), Mr. L. H. Bond, Miss Margo Tate (daughter of the headmaster of King's School) and Mrs. Edwards (wife of the manager of Ruston & Hornsby), a professional artist.

104.   A superb Walter Lee photograph of part of Grantham's Saturday market in the early 1950s. Except that some cottages have been replaced by Great Northern Court, little seems to have changed, though the market stalls of the 1990s are more modern.

105. The staff of Ruston & Hornsby Ltd. in 1925.

106. A group photograph at the Barracks in 1931. Posing here are the officers, warrant officers and sergeants of the local 'B' Company, 4th Battalion, Lincolnshire Regiment.

107.   Film star, Miss Anne Crawford, being presented with a bouquet at the June 1955 garden fête organised by the 7th Grantham St John's Scouts at 'Norman Leys' on Beacon Lane. Sadly Miss Crawford died the following year, at the age of 35, a victim of leukaemia.

108. A coronation festival poster, dated Thursday 28 June 1838, inviting the local population to a variety of entertainments including a dance on Wood Hill, now known as St Peter's Hill.

109. Grantham photographer, F. G. Simpson, took this splendid picture. Sadly, no-one seems to know why these people were gathered together, the girls in such beautiful hats.

110. The Market Place on 30 January 1901 when the townspeople assembled to hear the proclamation of the accession of H.M. King Edward VII read by the mayor of Grantham from the steps of the Aberdeen granite obelisk. This replaced the medieval market cross in August 1886.

111. A parade of ex-servicemen outside the Guildhall recruiting office. This photograph must have been taken before September 1939 because by then the Guildhall, together with other important buildings, had been sand-bagged for protection.

RUSTON AND HORNSBY'S BAND

Will generously give their services for

BARNARDO'S HOMES

(GRANTHAM Y.H.L. COT),

AT A

Musical Promenade

ON

Friday, July 22nd, 1921

IN THE GROUNDS OF

ELSHAM HOUSE

(Kindly lent by J. W. HORNSBY, Esq.)

COMPETITIONS, ETC., ETC.

ADMISSION, 6d.   6—9 P.M.

Printed at the Press of Dr. Barnardo's Homes

112.   Advertisement for a musical concert by the Ruston & Hornsby band.

113. In 1935 the Borough of Grantham celebrated its Civil Centenary, and Messrs. G. R. Burton & Son Ltd. of Swinegate won the Championship Cup for the finest window display. A shiny new Morris 10 is the centrepiece of the exhibition.

114. Grantham's own brewers, Mowbray & Co. Ltd., had six exhibits in the 'monster procession' that took place on Tuesday 18 June 1935 as part of the Civic Centenary celebrations. These two vehicles are parked next to the *Blue Horse* in London Road.

115. Never-to-be-repeated bargains of October 1968. The lure was the cheap sugar, especially useful in the early autumn for jam making.

116. The Saturday pig sale in the wide Westgate part of Grantham market was always an interesting sight. The market is not as lively or noisy now that pigs are sold at the weekly Thursday cattle market.

117. This Armistice Sunday parade took place in November 1954 with the colour party under the command of Mr. John Henry 'Jim' Norton, chairman of the local branch of the 'Old Contemptibles'. Mr. Horace Hawks is the colour bearer and the colour escort includes Sergeants McWilliams and Lovell, and Corporal Knapp – all members of the 4th/6th Battalion, Royal Lincolnshire Regiment.

Richard Hornsby and Sons

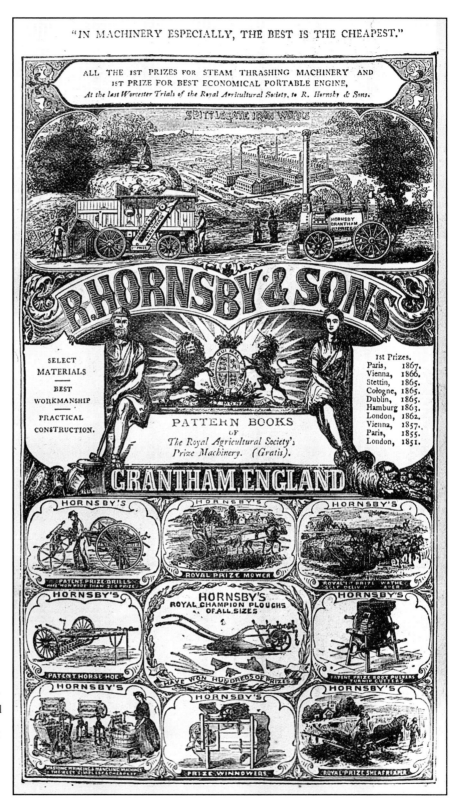

118. The inside back cover of an 1867 Hornsby catalogue. 'All the 1st Prizes for Steam Thrashing Machinery, and 1st Prize for the Best Economical Portable Engine, At the last Worcester trials of the Royal Agricultural Show to R. Hornsby & Sons.'

119. It is well known locally that Hornsby's invented the track. This photograph shows a Hornsby engine with tracks pulling a heavy load over a ditch. It is one of many photographs taken during various demonstrations for the benefit of the War Office up to 1908. The War Office was not impressed.

120. A 40-h.p. Rochet-Schneider motor car, also with a heavy load, successfully crossing 20 ft. of sand.

121. Eventually Hornsby's was large enough to provide many of the facilities required by a busy factory, for example a fire brigade. This photograph, taken by Simpson of Wharf Road, is not dated but was probably taken in the late 1890s.

122. Another pre-1900 view of Hornsby's fire brigade.

123. During the First World War Hornsby's produced munitions. As many of the workers had joined up, their places were taken by women.

HORNSBY'S F.C., 1916-17.

Back Row: R. Parker.   H. Digby.   R. Marvin.   B. Alcock.   W. Swain.   H. Batty.
Middle Row: W. Goodley.   N. Pinchbeck.   W. Partridge.
Front Row: W. Ifould.   C. Christopher.   F. Watchorn.   S. Preston.   T. Bullock.

124. Sport continued despite the war. Presumably these young men were not old enough for the forces or had reserved occupations in 1917. There are some well-known local names among the players, such as Swain, Pinchbeck, Watchorn and Batty.

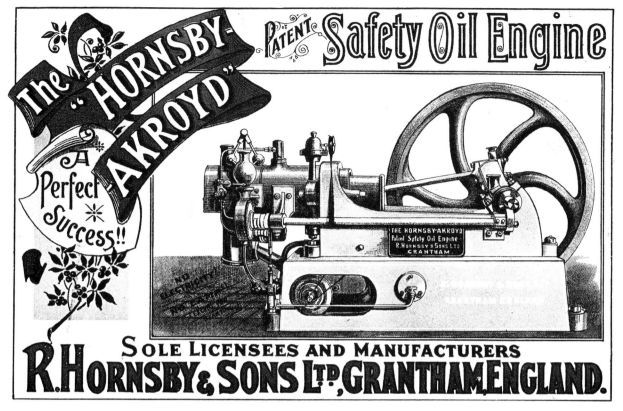

125.   The 'Hornsby Ackroyd' engine of 1892, 'a perfect success', was the forerunner of many such designs in later years. Another advertisement claimed that the engine required 'no driver, no boiler, no gas, no coal, no chimney, no steam and no water consumed'. It used 'cheap common oil' and cost less than ½d. per indicated horse power per hour to run.

126.   'The Paint Field', c.1890. Hornsby thrashing machines are in the foreground, and binders are being loaded on to the Great Northern Railway wagons. The location can be pinpointed by the South Parade railway bridge and the Great North Road seen on the left.

The following photographs, not precisely dated, are of various parts of the large, busy and cluttered Hornsby factory. The unknown photographer has captured for all time the many aspects of heavy engineering. The grime of the foundry, the noise of the machine shops and the danger of the miles of whirling belts can be imagined.

127. The Pattern Shop.

128. The Bottom Foundry where agricultural and small engine components were cast.

129.   No. 13 Shop. The heavy machine bay.

130.   A very tidy view of the Brass Gallery where the brass castings were machined.

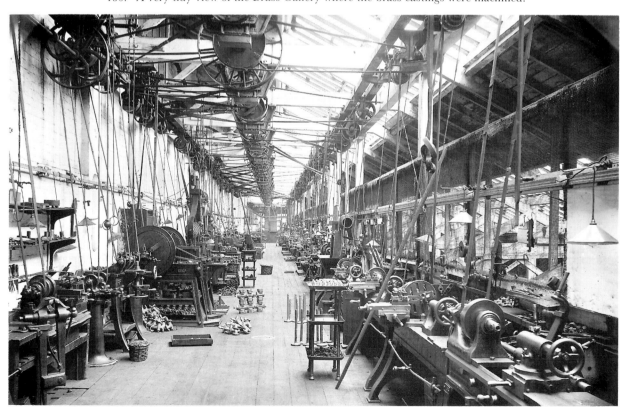

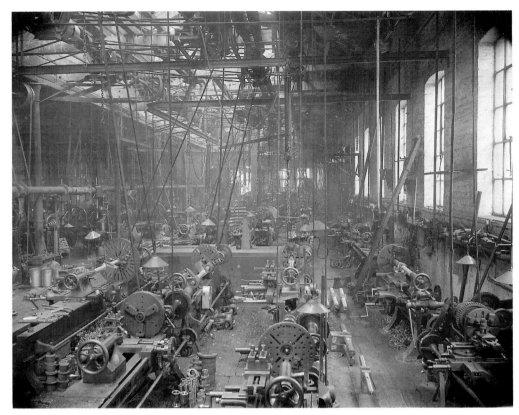

131. No. 14 Shop. This was where the much heavier crankshafts were machined – some can be seen on the floor.

132. No. 15 Shop. The drilling section.

133. The Packing Shop. This opened on 1 March 1905 and superseded the area shown in plate 126.

134. A memorial card to the founder of this great factory and the man who, more than anyone else, changed Grantham from a small market town to a thriving industrial town.

In Affectionate Remembrance

of

Richard Hornsby,

WHO DEPARTED THIS LIFE JANUARY 6TH, 1864,

AGED 73 YEARS.

Street Scenes

135.   Harrison's shop in Watergate, decorated to celebrate Queen Victoria's diamond jubilee in 1897. The patriotic message is a typical expression of the confidence of late Victorian England. A good selection of Harrison's wicker chairs can be seen under the archway.

136.　A wintry view of St Peter's Hill and the Frederick Tollemache statue.

137.　Another view of St Peter's Hill, showing the other statue and the fairly new Guildhall. The Newton statue was erected in 1857 when 'The Wilderness', as it was then known, was converted into 'the green' we know today.

138. An unmetalled Castlegate, showing the ancient *Beehive* public house. The signboard reads:

'Stop Traveller, this wondrous sign explore,
And say when thou has viewed it o'er and o'er
Grantham now two rarities are thine,
A lofty steeple and a living sign.'

The 'living sign' is a beehive, complete with bees, resting in a tree outside the public house.

139. The wide part of Westgate looking even wider than it does today because of the absence of the motor car.

140. The Skegness lifeboat passing along Wharf Road in 1906. This parade was part of a fund-raising exercise. The boat has just passed the Baptist church (left of photograph) and the *Musicians Arms* (on the right). The two top-hatted gentlemen in the carriage are Dr. Richard Wilson on the left and Father Sabela, the Roman Catholic priest, on the right.

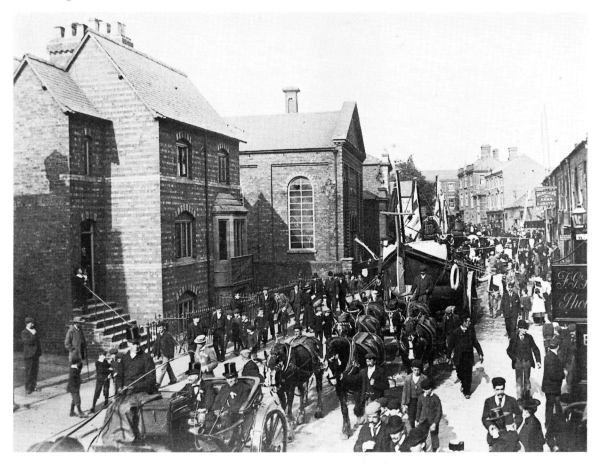

141. Another photograph which shows how the magnificent spire and tower of St Wulfram's church dominated the old town centre. This is a view of Vine Street, before it was truncated by the widening of Watergate in 1948.

142. Vine Street after the *Cross Swords* was closed in 1958.

143. Swinegate in August 1902, celebrating the coronation of Edward VII.

144. St Peter's Hill and High Street on 'Mafeking Day' in 1900. The white house on the right was replaced by the present-day Lloyd's Bank building.

145. A much later view of St Peter's Hill and High Street showing two of Grantham's former cinemas, the Granada and the Picture House, both long since gone.

146. Manthorpe Road decorated for the coronation of King George V and Queen Mary in 1911. The *Three Crowns*, on the left, was closed in 1931. The nearest houses on the right have been replaced by a petrol filling station.

147.   An inter-war view of what is now known as 'Gainsborough Corner'. This is the south end of London Road.

148.   A 1929 view of Old Wharf Road which led from Wharf Road to the canal basin and Grantham's first railway station.

149.   In this photograph the top of Watergate has been widened and the bottom part is ready for redevelopment. In fact it was not redeveloped and remains a car park to this day.

150.   By the 1960s things were changing. Here the Picture House site is for sale. The building was replaced by an unimaginative Tesco store.

151.   In this photograph of March 1961 more buildings, including the stone *Horse and Jockey*, are destined for demolition. Unusually, the *Horse and Jockey* did not face on to the Great North Road, later High Street. Entrance was through a side door.

152. A superb action scene of a horse sale in wide Westgate, probably in the 1890s. The barber's pole on the left belonged to S. Cant, hairdresser, and Mr. and Mrs. Brown were proprietors at the *Blue Bull* for many years.

153.　One of the earliest photographs of the Market Place, taken between 1872 and 1882, before the market cross was removed for the second time.

154.　A post-1904 view of the Market Place. The cross has been removed and replaced by the Aberdeen granite obelisk. Notice the post office on the left.